Miracle in Santarém

THREADS OF
gold

An inspiring true story of hope,
courage, forgiveness, and grace.

DANI O'DELL

WAUTHORSUNITE

Cover by Sylvia Sutliff
Interior Formatting by Kurt Dierking II

ISBN: 978-1-960346-60-5

Miracle in Santarém

THREADS OF
gold

An inspiring true story of hope,
courage, forgiveness, and grace.

DANI O'DELL

AUTHORSUNITE

Table of Contents

Author's Preface   1

CHAPTER I
Miracle in Santarém – 1247 AD   5
Chapter I: Reflection Questions   15

CHAPTER II
A Lesson in Hope   27
Chapter II: Reflection Questions   33

CHAPTER III
A Lesson in Courage   45
Chapter III: Reflection Questions   55

CHAPTER IV
A Lesson in Forgiveness   67
Chapter IV: Reflection Questions   75

CHAPTER V
A Lesson in Grace   87
Chapter V: Reflection Questions   99

Acknowledgments   111

Bibliography   115

About the Author   119

Photos of Santarém   120

.

Author's Preface

For as long as I can remember, miracles have captured my heart—especially the little ones. Like having to turn back to get the keys, only to see the important papers we forgot or that extra pause at a stop light that keeps us from the accident ahead. In these grace-filled moments, we have had the gift of setting our world right and to begin again.

I would like to say these reminders always slow me down, completely in awe of the extraordinary workings of our universe. It feels like only a blink, though, is spent in gratitude before I am caught up again in the busyness of the day. No, it is only in those times that I consciously slow down, take a breath, and take in the breadth of the beauty of our world that the magnitude of the miracles, great and small, all around us truly changes me. Albert Einstein once said,

"There are only two ways to live your life. One is as though nothing is a miracle. The other is as though everything is."

When we get caught up in the wonder of our universe, our lives change because we are changed. We become curious as to how these events occur, who or what orchestrates them, why they occur and if there is a design at the core.

Miracles have an intrinsic faith and hope embedded within them beckoning us to question and, ultimately, believe that there is more to this life and our world than what we can physically see. Philosophers, theologians, scientists, scholars, and masses of humanity have wrestled with these questions since the beginning of time and yet, the grandeur of the workings of this world remains ever elusive.

My faith is Catholic, so I was brought up hearing story upon story of miracles throughout history. This fueled my fascination for the unexplainable and still fuels it today. In that unexplainable I hope to ignite a spark of hope that we are here for a reason, that there is something (and in my case, someone) out there that loves us beyond our comprehension, and we are worthy to receive that love. In the chaos that has been in our world from the beginning, we must discern our path to love, choose daily to follow that path and to regain our balance when we fall. Too many are lost and defeated because love has been lost or is buried under the burdens we carry.

I believe if we graciously embrace the lessons along our path to receive even a shred of hope for that love, it is better than no hope. So, on the following pages I share a miracle that touched me to my core. It has led me to explore and appreciate history, faith, love, and our humanity.

We, together in love, whatever our faith, can lift each other up and find purpose in every breath we take. I pray we all receive the grace to be a part of this loving connection.

Chapter 1
Miracle in Santarém
1247 AD

Maria's Challenge

In the year 1247 AD, a peasant woman living in the town of Santarém, Portugal was struggling with the unfaithfulness of her husband. As a peasant woman in the Middle Ages there were very few options open to her. Divorce was not common for peasants and as the story is told, the woman, who we will call Maria[1], only wanted her husband's love and not to lose him altogether.

A common option at that time was to visit a local soccer, or sorceress, to cure and solve problems. Whether it was poor crops, the need for rain, a sick family member or even that unfaithful spouse, many believed these soccers[2] could help and heal those in need. So, Maria summoned up her courage and paid the town soccer a visit.

---

[1] The names of the couple could not be verified, so to personalize the experiences of the couple, we have given the woman the common Portuguese name, Maria, and her husband the common Portuguese name, Pedro.

[2] The terms soccer and sorceress are used interchangeably.

The Communion Host

The item requested by the soccer for the return of her husband's love was for Maria to steal a consecrated Communion host[3] from church. To steal a consecrated host was not taken lightly back then and would not be taken lightly today. Maria was Catholic and in the Catholic faith, it is taught that during the Liturgy of the Mass through a process called transubstantiation, the host becomes the body, blood, soul, and divinity of Christ. Catholics receive Communion to receive Jesus, and in doing so prayerfully bring his presence into our bodies and thus into the world. It is a complex subject, and it is not known if Maria fully understood this belief. But, from what is known, she knew enough to hesitate at the proposition from the soccer.

Regardless of her hesitation, she eventually went to St. Stephen's Catholic Church, her parish, a short two blocks from the local soccer. After receiving Holy Communion, instead of placing the consecrated host into her mouth, she hid it in her scarf with the intention of taking it to the sorceress. As she left the church many people were outside enjoying each other's company. Their eyewitness account of what happens next marks the start of the first miracle.

---

[3] A Communion host is a small round piece of flat bread.

The Miracle

As Maria walked down the last church step and headed in the direction of the sorceress, she could feel moisture in her hand that was holding the scarf. Looking down she could see blood flowing from her scarf. The crowd outside of the church noticed, as well, and hurried to help her.

Not wanting anyone to know what she had done, Maria ran home as spots of blood hit the pavement. Once there, she hid the bleeding host in a wood chest safely in her bedroom.

Imagine the thoughts that
were going through her mind...

How and why could this host be
bleeding and what did it mean?

How was she going to explain
her intentions for taking the host?

Should she tell her husband...
or tell the priest?

The anxiety and uncertainty
must have been unbearable.

The Light

That night while she slept with her husband at her side, the miraculous host brought more intrigue as a bright light emanated from the chest so intensely that it woke them both. With her secret exposed, she told her husband the truth. As her story unfolded, the gravity of the choices they each made lay before them. Distraught at the consequences of both of their actions, they knelt before the dazzling, light-filled chest and prayed for forgiveness throughout the night, the brilliant glow never wavering as they kept vigil until mornings' light.

Faith Rising

As the sun rose over the horizon, the worried couple went to the church to receive guidance from the parish priest. News spread quickly around the small town and soon a crowd gathered in and around their humble home to see the miracle. All through the day, the light shone brightly from the wood chest while the host continued to bleed. The entire town came to pray at the couple's home as the miracle glowed in the warmth of the light. Finally, the priest, followed by the crowd, took the communion host back to the church. There he wrapped it in wax to stop the bleeding and placed it in the tabernacle.

Imagine the faith that was born through this miracle to those townspeople who were witness to its light. The teachings of their faith had an answer to the miracle. Ancient scripture tied their weekly Communion (breaking of the bread) at church to the breaking of the bread by Jesus at the Last Supper, just before His passion and crucifixion on the cross. In this connection, we are invited to be a part of Jesus' extraordinary love in which He ultimately sacrificed everything for us to forgive our sins. The depth of Jesus' Love for us is indisputable, and here was a sign of that unwavering love.

Within this miracle lay the faith needed to believe in the **overwhelming love** of a God who beckons us to trust him, to believe that He will be with us through all time, and to know that **He is working** against the forces of evil for our good.

Miracles like this give us the capacity to have that shred of hope that we **are loved beyond** our comprehension and that we **are worthy** to receive that love every day of our lives.

More Miracles

Many more miracles have been noted surrounding this host. One of the most unusual is said to have happened in the following century when the clergy went into the church to get ready for Mass. The wax encasement holding the host was found shattered into pieces with the communion host now in a crystallized form. The clergy placed the mysterious crystal in a gold and silver monstrance where it remains displayed above the altar today. Royalty has venerated the miracle and studies have been conducted by clergy and scientists alike for over 700 years. In each of these studies, the authentication of the blood within the host has been confirmed as human blood. Through the studies performed authenticating the blood, the world has attempted to find some scientific explanation for the miracle, but none have been found to date.

Forever Love

In the humble, little town of Santarém, the church has been renamed The Church the Holy Miracle and the home of the couple has since been turned into a convent, The Chapel of the Miracle. Every second Sunday of April since the time of the original miracle, there has been a procession from the home-turned-convent to the church to honor this extraordinary event of abiding and steadfast love.

Thousands of pilgrims have **made their way** to the peaceful, little town filled with cobblestone streets to pay homage and, also to **contemplate the mystery** born centuries before of a poor, peasant woman with a **hope for love.**

Chapter 1:
Reflection Questions

1. Imagine being in Maria's or her husband's place that first night as the mysterious host was illuminated by the brilliant light.

    What thoughts and emotions do you think filled their hearts as they kept vigil? Reflect on each and share your insights on how you might have responded in their situation.

2. How do you think this experience impacted the faith of the townspeople witnessing the miraculous light surrounding the host?

   Consider how this event might have deepened their belief in God's incomprehensible love. What lasting effects do you think this miracle had on their lives?

3. Reflect on any miracles you or someone close to you have experienced. Did these events lead to unexpected outcomes?

   If so, how have these outcomes shaped or changed your life? Has this story influenced the way you view the miracles in your own life?

4. Have you ever held onto secrets so tightly that even those closest to you were unaware of your struggles?

   Reflect on a time when you felt as desperate as Maria did when her life did not go as planned. How did you navigate those feelings?

5. Think of a time when you shared your needs with someone and were unexpectedly met with understanding and love.

   How did this experience change your perspective on being open and vulnerable?

Chapter 11
A Lesson in Hope

Moving Mountains

Every human encounter holds lessons, and this miracle is no exception. Although set in the Middle Ages, nuggets of valuable and practical insights for our own journey can be unearthed. In this story, Maria came upon a crossroads in her life and needed to be brave or her life would be filled with regret and suffering. We, like Maria, all face challenges in life in which the daily choices we make are pivotal to our well-being. Each action we make propels us towards or away from the life we want. For Maria, as a peasant woman in the Middle Ages, pain and suffering were a part of life. There were no other avenues, no freedom to choose another path, so Maria's bravery and resolve to find a solution was very special, very out of the ordinary, and very filled with the hope necessary to move mountains in her world.

Every one of us at some point in our lives has something that feels as insurmountable as Maria's challenge to overcome. Whether illness, loss, or an obstacle that holds us far from our goals, sometimes hope is the only thread that keeps us moving forward to one day grasp the extraordinary on the other side.

Much of the reason for Maria's steadfast resolve was the culture and beliefs of Western Europe at the time. Royalty and peasants alike had strong faith communities in the Christian Church from which hope sprung from the pulpit during every sermon. Jesus' teachings of love, justice, wisdom, and prudence resonated with a people wanting to bring order and civility to a chaotic world. The Catholic Church was the only Christian Church at the time and its moral convictions of caring for the sick, elderly, women and children tugged on the consciousness of mankind. Its arguments made sense to rulers and monarchs of much of Europe and slowly, gradually from the barbaric violence of the Dark Ages, a new chivalrous existence began to emerge.

Hope in Action

Maria was born and raised in an era when kings would hold counsel with Church leaders on policy, so there was a moral unity of spirit, mind and governing. The Bible teachings of love, justice and human dignity were spreading throughout Europe and a hope for dignity of all life was blossoming. Thus, Maria found herself in a time where even a peasant woman could hope for a better life. Her daily life was filled with a community who cared for each other and prayed devoutly. She had been taught of the love of Jesus, of His miracles, and of the people He healed. She knew of His own suffering on the cross, His resurrection, and of the everlasting life that He promised. Within that promise a hope was born in the hearts and minds of a new generation that would propel society to greater heights in human dignity, honor, and respect.

History does not record for us how strong a faith Maria had or how much she believed this narrative was true. It is not known how much was only hope in the love and respect promised in these teachings, just as hope is hidden in the hearts and minds of each one of us. The intermingling of full belief and glimpses of hope teeters back and forth for us, as we, like Maria, venture through our lives making sense of our own dignity, moral character and choices that will dictate our legacy for a world that so desperately needs people of strong character to guide it.

Transformation Through Hope

What we do know is that hope is a precious virtue and valuable trait to carry and protect, for without it, despair in our suffering can take over our lives. All the beauty, creativity, and love that we bring into this world can be lost when we lose hope. We must model Maria, the peasant woman, who was given the gift of hope in her heart. This hope propelled her to search for a love that she knew existed and it can propel us, as well. With determination in the face of challenges and temptations, Maria embarked on a journey that transformed her whole being. She came away with not only the love she was hoping for on the other side, but with a miraculous, tangible sign of the divine love waiting for each of us.

This sign sits humbly above the altar of the Church of the Most Holy Miracle, silently comforting and beckoning us all and generations of pilgrims that visit to contemplate its mysteries.

Chapter 11:
Reflection Questions

1. Consider the challenges in your life where your daily choices have been pivotal to your well-being. Can you identify specific choices that have helped you move closer to your goals?

   Conversely, what choices have set you back? Reflect on how these decisions have impacted your journey.

2. Think of a time when hope gave you strength to overcome significant obstacles.

    How did your belief in your ability to achieve your goal shape the way you approached the challenge? Did this belief make a difference in the outcome?

3. Reflect on a time when you lost hope during a difficult situation? How did this loss affect your sense of beauty, creativity and love? What kinds of obstacles contributed to your loss of hope, and how did they impact your life?

    Has hope alone ever brought you to the love or goal you were looking for on the other side? What are some of your examples?

4. Has hope ever been the sole factor that helped you achieve something extraordinary?

    What beliefs did you hold about reaching that goal and how did those beliefs influence your success?

5. Do you believe that the challenges you've faced have led to personal growth and transformation? Reflect on the wisdom you've gained from these experiences?

   How has this wisdom changed your perspective on hope and its role in your life? Do you believe that the struggle to overcome the challenge was necessary for the growth and transformation you received?

Chapter III
A Lesson in Courage

Where Does Courage Sit?

For Maria the virtue of courage was paramount in obtaining her dream of regaining the love of her husband. We do not know what type of relationship Maria and her husband, Pedro, had. But what we do know is that in the Middle Ages it was common for love to be at the core of peasant relationships. There were no property prizes, as in the upper class, to obtain from selecting a wife, so there was a strong possibility the two were in love when they married. They were brought up with a moral conscience of Christian teachings that the marital act outside of marriage was sinful, so we can surmise the betrayal they both knew lay at the foundation of Pedro's infidelity.

The difficult part
about courage is that it,
like every other virtue we seek,
is set precariously in the
middle ground between
two opposing vices.

When approaching the courageous choice, we wrestle with the consequences of reckless action or, the extreme opposite, debilitating non-action. By trial and error, we find where courage sits. Sometimes we recklessly go too far, sometimes we do not do enough. We must go through this process because through it we gain insight and wisdom in knowing when to push our boundaries out of our comfort zone or to pull back when we go too far.

The Power of Courage

Maria's moral compass for her courage boundaries came from the beliefs and daily routines in her life. The town in which she lived, Santarém, Portugal, had been a fortress city in its earliest days with King Alfonso I, Portugal's king, fighting valiantly for Christianity in the region. Courage and victory were tangible. Peasants in the 13th century saw that courage could bring about change and that they had the power to be a part of that change. Courageous action begets more courageous action and Maria believed that fighting boldly for her love could right her world. Although she stumbled through reckless actions along the way, the divine shone a miracle upon her life that became a legacy of love the world will never forget.

We, too, must find our **courage boundaries.**

We must allow ourselves to stretch out of our comfort zones and to also **push ourselves** when we are immobilized by fear and indecision.

Without consciously doing both things, we cannot find our own unique **courage sweet spot.**

Finding Our Unique Genius

In this legacy we are drawn into the conversation of what our place is in the grand scheme. Our place is undeniably special and unquestionably unique. No two people will ever want or need the same things or have the same gifts. These differences define us, yet connect us in a beautiful design, which, when completed leads us to a world filled with a grace we could not achieve on our own.

We each have something unique to give the world, but many of us leave this earth without realizing the full breadth of our purpose. We must have the courage to find our uniqueness, to seek out the things that bring us joy and that bring joy into our world.

The truth in this statement could not be more evident than in the humble, seemingly insignificant life of Maria. Her desire to be loved by the husband who vowed his fidelity was filled with purity and promise. Her courage to persevere and find her way to love, noble. The entire process she went through to come to the fruit of the miracle is not known, but she persevered, and, in the end, her unique genius shone brightly.

The Power of Prayer

It is easy to busy and distract ourselves with things that don't matter instead of finding the courage and focus to pursue what will bring us peace. Discovering what does and doesn't matter to come to that peace takes continual internal reflection. So, we, like Maria, can learn to be noble, steadfast, and courageous. And ultimately, we, like Maria, can find our peace. We must take the time for this internal reflection. We must discern what our own needs, desires, and talents are, so we, too, can bring our best into the world.

Moments of silence and solitude keep us reflecting on and moving towards what is best for us and for the world around us. We find our way in these moments. A powerful form of silence and solitude is prayer, and prayers were an important part of daily life in the Middle Ages of Western Europe. Being a peasant in the Middle Ages meant prayers to God for everything. Prayers for meals, prayers for marriage, prayers for birth, prayers for crops, prayers for prosperity, health, and love. Within these prayerful moments, Maria went inside herself to build up her courage muscle and her moral conscience of right living. She sought wisdom for the needs of her heart by reflecting on Jesus' teachings of respect, love, and peace strengthening her resolve. This resolve, both hopeful and courageous, brought about a miracle that has remained unexplained for over 700 years.

We do not know what beauty lies within us without taking the time to go within to search for it. Our incredible genius, and gift to the world around us, can only come from truly understanding our own unique needs, desires, and talents. In Matthew Kelly's, *The Rhythm of Life*, he nudges us to do just that and contemplate the invaluable genius and gifts within each of us. By reflection we come to know ourselves, so we can give the world what it needs from us and, in return, humbly receive what we need from the world.

By working towards creating a life where our needs, desires and talents live in harmony, we come closer to living our fulfilled, purposeful life and can attain the love that is waiting for us.

The Courageous Life

In his opening address for The Ethics of Courage at The Ethics Centre, Dr. Matthew Beard is quoted as saying:

To live is to have a nerve constantly exposed to the world - always vulnerable to suffering.

What a daunting statement.
We are vulnerable to suffering
- whether we take risks or stay paralyzed in fear –
just by being alive.

In this vulnerability, it is much easier to complain, become anxious and to spin on our thoughts than it is to do something about it. But when we remember that courage to do what is right takes both inner action and outer action, our way forward becomes less intimidating. With reflection (the inner action) we can see the path (outer action) we must take before we take it.

Prayer brings about that visualization of our hopes and dreams. It has no fear because we are our most courageous selves in the solitude of our minds. With prayer, we can see the best way forward.

The courageous life may be more difficult, it may take **more prayer, more discernment, and more grit,** but it, also, ultimately leads to the very life we were created for.

Chapter III:
Reflection Questions

1. Reflect on a challenging time when you acted impulsively or were paralyzed by fear?

    How do your emotions influence the way you confront a challenge? What role do they play in your decision making?

2. Do you feel you've discovered your "courage sweet spot" —a balance between fear and excessive risk-taking?

   Have you gained insight and wisdom from pushing yourself out of your comfort zone during challenges? If so, what steps have helped you reach your goals?

3. Have you considered what makes you unique and what brings you joy?

    Take a moment to jot down five or six qualities or characteristics that define who you are and make you uniquely you.

4. Do you believe that prayer can guide you in visualizing the best path forward when facing challenges?

   How does prayer help you discern the way to peace and achieving your goals?

5. Think of a time when a challenge prevented you from pursuing something you wanted.

   Can you see how being hopeful and courageous either helped you achieve your goal or could have changed the outcome? How do you think hope and courage can impact your life?

Chapter IV
A Lesson in Forgiveness

We All Could Use a Little Mercy

If anyone struggled with the complexities of forgiveness, it was Maria. First, she was betrayed by her husband and had to come face to face with her own anger, resentment, and bitterness. She then had to move past her anger and into forgiveness to find the love that was buried beneath it. Next, she had to come to terms with her own immeasurable betrayal towards her Creator by her own actions when she stole the consecrated host. Instead of retaliating in anger, God gave her a sign of His overwhelming love for her. He reminded her that He was there for her and would be for all time.

Maria and her husband, Pedro, were both humbled profoundly. They each had to face their own errors in judgment and betrayal. They each needed forgiveness for their own actions.

To be human is to be imperfect. The humbling truth of it is that we all falter.

Our Own Worst Enemy?

Life is an interesting classroom, isn't it? We all feel anger, betrayal and rightful resentment for things that have happened to us. We sometimes choose to hold onto that resentment for our entire lives and many times, the world agrees with our righteousness in that decision. But who does that resentment hurt the most? And at what cost does that resentment come?

We know, logically, that holding onto anger hurts us the most because, at its seeming worst, it can consume our every waking moment. But worse yet, it does more damage. It keeps us from sleeping and creeps into our daily actions with others, poisoning the relationships we hold most dear. We are the ones taken over by sadness, fear, and anger. We are the ones bringing that bitterness into our relationships and we are the ones not reaching our potential because we are so tired, we have no more to give.

Then there is the unquantifiable cost. All the hours of negative thoughts and behaviors steal the very happiness, creativity, and love that we feel we lost from the negative experience. The paradox is discouraging. *So how do we move past the hurt to get out of this negativity?*

Letting Go

Maria teaches us another lesson here. She made a conscious decision to forgive her husband and move forward to hold her marriage together.[4] Depending on the facts involved, in another case the prudent decision may have been to end the marriage for the infidelity. The discernment process in this decision should not be taken lightly, because for some the best choice would be to leave. The focus we are noting here, though, is not whether they stayed together, but rather that Maria made a conscious decision to let go of her anger and move forward with that decision. Without that conscious decision to let go and move forward, she could have spent a lifetime in anguish, anger, and bitterness, forever stuck in the mire of unworthiness. Instead, she chose to move from anger to compassion for her husband and, equally as important, for herself. Forgiveness is not just an act of compassion to the offending party, but an act of compassion to ourselves, as well.

[4] Historical note: It is not definitively known whether Maria and Pedro were ultimately able to save their marriage, although it seems more likely following the miracle they both witnessed. What is known is that they were profoundly impacted in a positive way from the miracle.

When we can give others and
ourselves compassion,
we ease our own suffering.

When we ease our suffering,
we bring more peace
and love to our lives
and the lives around us.

It is in that peace and love
that we live our best lives.

It is in that peace that we can
visualize a path forward.

A Crack in Our Armor

The funny thing about how upset we can get about someone else's transgressions is how lightly we can excuse our own offenses. Maria had to have known she was doing something wrong when she took the consecrated host because she purposely hid it on the way out of the church. She excused her own wrongdoing because she was overcome with her own wants and rationalized her actions. We all do this in our daily lives. We can be filled with anger about what someone else has done but fail to realize the hurt that we have caused. This realization alone should start to open a channel to forgiveness for each of us. That is all we need, just a crack in our armor. This softening of our hearts always leads to internal peace and growth.

Jesus knew what would bring the most change in the world and chose peace daily. Mother Theresa, Dr. Martin Luther King Jr., Rosa Parks are all peace warriors that have made the decisive choice of love over hatred and these choices have altered our world forever. The existence of peace warriors throughout the worlds' history changes our thoughts, changes our lives and changes our legacies. Whether young or old, this growth in mercy brings wisdom into our lives and our world.

We must make a conscious
choice every day as to what
we will bring to the world.

Do we bring wisdom,
compassion and love or
do we bring hurt,
anger, and resentment?

The choice is ours.

Chapter IV:
Reflection Questions

1. Recall a time when you faced the challenge of forgiving someone who hurt you.

   What emotions did you need to— or still need to— work through to reach forgiveness? How has this process affected you?

2. Do you recognize how holding onto hurt can drain happiness, creativity and love from your daily life?

   How does developing compassion for yourself help you move forward in forgiving others?

3. How challenging is it for you to let go of anger?

   Do you see how choosing to move forward from anger can ease your own suffering and bring you peace?

4. Think of times when you were the one seeking forgiveness. How does it affect your life when you are met with love and compassion?

   How does it affect your life when you are met with anger and resentment? What impact does this have on your other relationships and your well-being?

5. Does this story help you understand the importance of opening yourself to forgiveness, even if just a little - that crack in your armor?

   Reflect on how different the world would be without peace warriors like Jesus, Mother Theresa, Dr. Martin Luther King Jr., and Rosa Parks. Do you see yourself growing in wisdom and compassion through this understanding?

Chapter V
A Lesson in Grace

Threads of Gold

This miracle brings with it a beautiful lesson in grace, as well. We are told that grace is given freely and unmerited, and that is evident in our story. We will probably never know why Maria was chosen for this particular miracle or how the miracle has remained all these years. What we do know is that grace weaved many beautiful stitches into the fabric of Maria's life that would change her forever. Grace is and always will be that very extraordinary happening when our life aligns perfectly. We feel it. There is flow in what we do, and we know that our world is steadied and right. Our hearts and our minds are filled with peace by that grace-filled, precious as gold moment.

We all long to stitch these golden threads together, moment by moment, knowing that each is a perfect gift. In Maria's longing, her first golden stitch filled her thoughts with unwavering hope. The second filled her heart with steadfast courage. The third stitch shone with bountiful mercy. Within the loom we see both the heartache and the triumph, the lessons and the wisdom, and, ultimately, an everlasting and undying love from her Creator. *Each golden stitch connecting her more fully to the unconditional love she was destined for.*

Opportunity's Door

Grace has a funny way of weaving golden threads into our lives when we are open to it. In 2022, I had the opportunity to visit The Church of the Holy Miracle in the charming city of Santarém, Portugal. I had read about the miracle earlier that year and was excited that a pre-planned trip had set me within a 45-minute drive to its door ~ my Golden Stitch Number One.

This is how my husband and I found ourselves twisting through cobblestone narrow streets lined with shops, making our way to the humble, stone-clad church that Maria attended. It was a very misty, overcast November day as we walked into the vestibule of the quiet church. We paused at each of the photographs on the wall hoping to glean more about the centuries old event. Not a soul was in the church, so we took our time in the silence, each in our own thoughts. After we took it all in, we ended up in a room that held both a display of historical church vestments, as well as, the gift shop. We had read that someone would be available for questions on the history of the church, so we were happy to see an elderly Portuguese woman behind the cash register speaking with a customer. Once she finished with the customer, we let her know of our interest in the Miracle of Santarém. With her apology in Portuguese, thoughts of a thorough history lesson quickly evaporated. *Uh oh... now what!?!*

As One Door Closes Another Opens

As we turned to each other for our next steps, the gentleman she had been speaking to graciously...*and* in English... asked us to wait a moment.

This gentleman, Luis, turned out to be an English-speaking tour guide, commissioned by a famous priest from Mexico. Here he was with the priest and a small film crew, busy relaying to his client in Spanish the story that had fascinated me that whole past year.

Luis took us up to a door leading behind the altar. As we entered the back room, he touched a very tiny, elderly gentleman on the shoulder...speaking in Portuguese to him ...and told us to follow the gentleman. As Luis quickly went back out to join his client, the elderly man proceeded to walk us around the back side of the altar where there was a very old, very thin wooden ladder. He gestured for us to proceed up the ladder. It wasn't until I took my first step on the ladder that I realized within a few moments I would be inches away from the host that touched Maria's life so many years before.

776 Years of Love

I finished climbing up the ladder to see a beautiful gold and silver reliquary, the center of which held the miraculous host within a glass encasement displaying both the blood and the host. Clear as day, I could see the same amazing miracle that Maria held in her hand all those years ago. *Crazy to think here I was over 5,000 miles from home, directly in front of this ancient mystery.* I prayed on top of the fragile ladder viewing the altar and the church pews beyond it on the other side. I imagined all the people over the centuries who had come to sit in those same pews to pray in search of understanding, peace, and the love at the core of its presence. I stood for a long time filled with gratitude and awe that I was now part of that history ~ my Golden Stitch Number Two.

My husband finished his turn, and the reverent, elderly gentleman took us to the pews to the right of the altar while we waited for Luis to finish. As I looked up at the reliquary holding the host, I could not help but be fascinated by our timing. *What if we got here an hour later or an hour earlier? Luis may not have been here, and this may have been the closest we would ever be to viewing the mysterious host— not the inches away that we had been on top of that ladder.* This was one of those moments that I consciously slowed down, took a breath, and took in the breadth of the beauty of our world.

The Story Retold

Luis came back to us after finishing with his guest, ready to answer any questions. He filled in the blanks and questions we had, bringing the story to life. The names of the husband and wife who turned Maria and Pedro's home into the convent in 1663 were Manuel dos Reis Tavares and Margarido Cesar de Almeida. He said the convent was only a two-minute walk down the street and then to the right. Pointing in another direction four minutes down the street and to the left, next to Graca Church, he said we could find the home of the sorceress.

We decided to walk the short two minutes in the light rain to Maria and Pedro's home. As we walked the narrow streets, I thought about how fearful Maria must have been as she hurried home with the Host bleeding in her hands. Turning the corner on the street to our destination, we could see the homes on either side of the couples' house were simple, white stucco buildings with window boxes filled with flowers lining each upper window. I could feel the presence of those devout, early Christians who had to make sense of the miracle in their midst.

Upon reaching the convent itself, we could see that it had been adorned on both sides with beautiful stone pillars and two oversized, dark-stained wood front doors. We noticed atop it all was a bell to ring in the hours. I could picture it ringing every second Sunday in April as the townspeople made their way through these same streets honoring that moment in 1246 AD.

There were no monstrous buildings or statues and, to be honest, the humbleness of the surroundings felt right. The simplicity intensified the love and mystery that had been brought to the small village some 700 years before, in my mind mirroring the same simplicity of Jesus' birth. I smiled thinking how beautiful it was that this mysterious story even brought two people from the United States almost halfway around the world to this very spot centuries later to contemplate the miraculous love witnessed here ~ my Golden Stitch Number Three.

Staying Forever Curious

Learning about the Eucharistic miracles sprinkled throughout history, some even in recent times, hits us profoundly because they inspire us to believe in the purest of love. They prod us to be curious and to ponder the wonder that is our world, and the love that we can find in it if we are open to it. Not only in these stories, but in the threads of the miracles of our everyday lives, the glints of grace-filled gold are there to be treasured and explored. These treasures call us to be hopeful, courageous, and forgiving while weaving our way towards love. Even if just for a moment, we receive that hope; that courage; and that mercy, like Maria, our lives will be forever altered by the moment and our next step forward will be redefined. It is in that redefinition that we right our world.

In his book, *A Cardiologist Examines Jesus*, the Italian cardiologist, Dr. Franco Serafini, reviews the testimonies of hematologists, oncologists, neurologists, geneticists, and molecular biologists who have studied Eucharistic miracles. It is a fascinating book. He analyzes the facts with a scientific eye bringing to light the frailties of the studies, as well as the unarguable truths found within each miracle.

Science and religion have been torn apart in our modern world, but the study of these miracles by renowned scientists has roused renewed interest in the intersection of the two. The researchers highlighted in Dr. Serafini's work, using advanced medical and forensic technology, have uncovered evidence supporting the authenticity of the tissue and blood found in these miracles. The samples analyzed contain tissue from a human heart, specifically the left ventricle myocardium, the most stressed muscle during cardiac trauma. Remarkably, the tissue shows signs of acute trauma, including inflammation and the presence of white blood cells indicating that the heart tissue was alive at the moment it was sampled – something science simply cannot explain as these samples were sometimes tested centuries after the fact. Additionally, the blood type identified in multiple Eucharistic miracles is AB, the same blood type found on relics believed to be the blood of Jesus. Could these tiniest of molecules weave the two disciplines together and beg us to explore them in unity? Much more scientific study needs to occur, but time will tell.

Perfecting Our Virtue Muscles

Within the unexplainable, the miraculous and the mysterious beauty in this story, and in all around us, I hope to ignite curiosity, interest, and study. Instead of shrugging things off because we are too busy, I hope we pause to learn more, love more, and understand more about our humanity.

More than ever, humanity needs to believe we each are worthy of love, that we can choose daily to follow the path to love and that we must regain our balance when we fall. There are so many uncontrollable tragic events around us, but one thing in our control is our ability to love. Hope, courage, and mercy are perfect virtue muscles to strengthen as we grow in love. Each difficulty before us gives us an opportunity to grow and learn. If we are open, there is no end to our learning and growth.

Fully understanding and living Jesus' commandment in John 15:12,

"Love one another as I have loved you," may be a task we never fully master, but in the living towards that growth in love, we become open to a very special, very unique, grace-filled life.

Connected in Love

And so, I end with my prayer posed in the preface:

May we, **together in love,**
whatever our faith,
lift each other up,
and **find purpose** in every
breath we take.
I pray we all **receive the grace**
to be a part of this
loving connection.

Chapter V:
Reflection Questions

1. Can you connect with the heartache and triumph, lessons and wisdom, and, ultimately, the love and grace Maria experienced within her loom of golden stitches?

    Share examples of challenging times when grace has weaved golden stitches in your life?

2. Have you ever been struck by how perfectly events can align as everything seems to flow effortlessly into place?

    How often do you take a moment to pause and appreciate the beauty within these moments? How do these experiences make you feel about the presence of grace in your life?

3. Have you ever encountered stories of Eucharistic miracles before, or is this a new concept for you?

   Does learning about them spark a desire to explore their significance and the messages they carry? Does it make you more curious about the significance and messages of the miracles within your own daily life?

4. How do you feel about the merging of science and religion, particularly as technology reveals astonishing details about the tissue and blood found in Eucharistic miracles?

What impact does this have on your understanding of grace?

5. Think of a time when you shared your needs with someone and were unexpectedly met with understanding and love.

How did this experience change your perspective on being open and vulnerable?

Acknowledgments

My golden threads contributing to this book...

To my parents, who first instilled in me the drive to seek out the virtues of hope, courage, mercy and grace.

To Matthew Kelly, for all his works, especially his insightful book, *Rhythm of Life*, which set me on the path of exploring buried aspects of my own unique genius in 2017.

To Father Michael Schmitz and Tim Hall, who gifted me gold threads in 2022 that would eventually lead to this book. Father Schmitz, for his homily on Eucharistic miracles that sparked my curiosity to study them, and Tim Hall, Personal Coach, whose guidance propelled me to step into the world of authorship.

To my sisters, Benita and Angela, who listened, daily at times, to every version of every chapter of this book and for being my earliest and biggest cheerleaders along the way.

To my husband, Dean, who believes I can do anything and loves me unconditionally...and who has listened to more readings of this book than anyone should have to.

To my children and children in love, Derek & Zara and Dena & Ryan, whose genuine appreciation for the essence of this book means more to me than I can ever express.

To Father Eugene, my pastor, who took the time out of his very busy life to sit with me, guide me and encourage me to pursue the publishing of this book.

To my friend, Jean Meronk, for her heartfelt edit—perfectly timed and insightfully given - thank you!

To all of my family, family-in-love, and friends who sat, listened, gave sage advice and even contacts, as well as, those who edited and encouraged me to get this series started and, who wholeheartedly support the messages within.

To all my "finishing touch" publishing threads...To my dear friend and gifted teacher, Cindy McFadden, who—while healing from a knee injury—happened to have the time to help with final edits. Timing is everything—Thank you!... To a couple very talented creatives: Dena, my daughter, who helped clear the cobwebs to shape the final vision of the cover, and Sylvia Sutliff, whose cover design work knocked it out of the park effortlessly. To Carlyn Craig at Post Hypnoticpress, thank you for bringing the audiobook version to life!...And to my wonderful publishing team, Nick Cass and Kurt Dierking at AuthorsUnite, for your patience, creative expertise, and commitment to preserving the heart of this book just as I envisioned it...you all amaze me!

To Derek, my son, without whose guidance, experience, creativity, and brilliant business sense I would probably never have gotten this project actually off the ground... thank you from the bottom of my heart for patiently acting as my agent while we navigate this new world of publishing.

To God, who in my belief, deserves all glory for all of our works.

...for all of this, I am deeply grateful.

Bibliography

Eucharistic Miracle in Santarem

Cruz, Joan Carroll. Eucharistic Miracles. TAN Books, 1987.

"Arautos do Evangelho." Eucharistic Miracle of Santarém. Arautos do Evangelho, https://www.arautos.org/os-milagres-catolicos/milagre-eucaristico-de-santarem. Accessed 16 March 2023.

Almeida, Paulo. "Relic of the Most Holy Miracle Santarém, Portugal." YouTube, uploaded by Paulo Almeida, 10 May 2023. (Tells the story of the miracle while getting video of the church and the miraculous host displayed above the altar.)

"The Incredible Eucharistic Miracle of Santarém." Catholic Life, Diocese of La Crosse, 15 April 2024, https://catholiclife.diolc.org/2024/04/15/the-incredible-eucharistic-miracle-of-santarem/. Accessed 20 May 2024.

"Chapel of the Miracle." Visit Portugal, Encyclopedia of Portuguese Localities. https://www.visitarportugal.pt/santarem/santarem/santarem/ermida-milagre. Accessed 20 May 2024. (Information on the home-turned-convent with information on the builders of the convent.)

Diocese of Santarém. "Sanctuary of the Most Holy Miracle." Diocese of Santarém, https://diocese-santarem.pt/santuario-do-santissimo-milagre/. (Official document from the Diocese of Santarem about the history of the miracle.)

Study of Other Eucharistic Miracles

Serafini, Franco, Dr. A Cardiologist Examines Jesus, The Stunning Science Behind Eucharistic Miracles. Sophia Institute Press, 2021.

"Miracle Hunter: A Cardiologist's Journey into Eucharistic Miracles." EWTN Vatican, https://www.ewtnvatican.com/articles/miracle-hunter-a-cardiologists-journey-into-eucharistic-miracles-1802/. Accessed 20 May 2024. (From an interview with Dr. Franco Serafini discussing his book on Eucharistic Miracles.)

Williams, Jeannette. "The Amazing Science of Recent Eucharistic Miracles: A Message from Heaven." Ascension Press, 3 November 2021, https://media.ascensionpress.com/2021/11/03/the-amazing-science-of-recent-eucharistic-miracles-a-message-from-heaven/. Accessed 15 May 2024.

Spitzer, Robert, S.J. Ph.D. "Contemporary Scientifically Validated Miracles Associated with Blessed Mary, Saints and the Holy Eucharist." Magis Center, 28 September 2017.

History, Virtue, Love and Life

Geary, Patrick J. "Peasant Religion in Medieval Europe." Cahiers d'Extreme-Asie, vol. 12, 2001, pp. 185-209.

Editors of Encyclopedia Britannica. "Afonso I, King of Portugal." Britannica, History and Society, Biography section, retrieved 8 August 2021.

Slattery, William J. Heroism and Genius: How Catholic Priests Helped Build—and Can Help Rebuild—Western Civilization. Ignatius Press, 2017.

Beard, Matthew. "Courage Isn't About Facing Our Fears, It's About Facing Ourselves." The Ethics Center, Opening address on The Ethics of Courage, 22 Aug. 2019.

Hermans, Kyle. "The Psychology of Courage: 7 Traits of Courageous Leaders." Forbes, 27 July 2022.

Kelly, Matthew. The Rhythm of Life: Living Every Day with Passion and Purpose. Blue Sparrow Books, 2018.

About the Author

Dani O'Dell lives in North Tustin, California with her husband, Dean, and their quirky dachshund, Joe—her loyal shadow.

Dani is a first-time author with a passion for sparking curiosity and reflection on the hope and love at the heart of miracles—not only in this story, but within our own lives.

She is currently working on *Miracle in Lanciano,* the second book in her Threads of *Gold series.*

To buy the book and learn more, visit: daniodell.com

Photos of Santarém

View from altar looking
at pews; October 2024.

Narrow cobblestone streets
of Santarém; October 2024.

View of the altar and host; October 2024.

The miraculous host; October 2024.

Father Niby and Dani O'Dell after Mass in front of the altar; October 2024.

Dani O'Dell in front of Maria's home turned convent; November 2022.